enough

AF365943

Taylor Koon

BookLeaf
Publishing

India | USA | UK

enough © 2024 Taylor Koon

All rights reserved.

No part of this publication may be reproduced, stored in a retrieval system, or transmitted, in any form or by any means, electronic, mechanical, photocopying, recording or otherwise, without the prior written permission of the presenters.

Taylor Koon asserts the moral right to be identified as author of this work.

Presentation by *BookLeaf Publishing*

Web: www.bookleafpub.com

E-mail: info@bookleafpub.com

ISBN: 9789363309593

First edition 2024

To my dear friends,

Thank you for being my home, my sanctuary, and my unwavering support. Your love and friendship have been the guiding light through my darkest days and the joy in my brightest moments. This book is for you.

With all my heart,

Taylor

Stay Small, Stay Here

the world is vast but I can't seem to feel the flow
the stream that will carry me to greater oceans

while we wait, fear creeps out of dark corners
it whispers

"stay small"
"stay here"

they try to take, to drown
while we fight to stay afloat

but staying for the sake of staying
will only hurt us both

and I yearn for home

Time

golden rays begin their roaming
gently stirring the world awake

for a moment everything is still
and anything is possible

I once thought freedom was wild, crazy,
constantly chasing
but now I see it is found in the calm, in the quiet

paths and twists stretch out into the light
and we learn that the destination is not the point

we have time
you have time

Anxious

3

an anchor weighs down into the depths
tied to my core, the current is too strong

to fight
to float

everything is dark and my vision blurs
as I struggle to make out faces

and no breath is satisfying
sunken, looking for the sky

how do I claw my way out?
which way is up?

Together Until the End

running hands over skin, feeling the curves
the bumps, the unfinished edges

always a work in progress
growing, stretching, changing

aging and freckles
wrinkles measuring a life

in laughter, in sorrow
in love

the relationship with the vessel
is ever-changing, like the tide

but she holds me, comforts me
together until the end

Bubbles

5

letting go
of pain
of expectations
sometimes of myself

to gulp the air
and feel bubbles find their way back up
light as laughter
I've never felt free like this before

and it tastes like comfort and excitement
can we always stay this way?

Solid Ground

you fall asleep
I tuck you in
I would do anything to keep you
singing, comfortable, happy

take any piece of me that you need
like tickets, there's a price
but you don't have to pay
this one's on me

and when I finally rest
as I leave this world
I hope that I leave solid ground
for someone else to stand on

Exist

it's natural
to take up the room, filling up every corner
energy bright and beautiful

but it's learned
to make yourself small
gathering handfuls of pieces of you

panic as you're
grasping and dropping
trying not to make a sound

but you can't leave quietly
and you don't want to make a scene
the Earth is screaming

until you finally find a room
that can handle the weight
allowing yourself to exist again

Whole Again

8

sometimes when people leave
it can feel like a part of you is ripping, tearing
taken

but peace is found
when you realize that you are already complete

anything added
is welcome excess

the unnecessary parts of you will regrow
and the day will come where
you will feel whole again

Poison

the world can set traps for us
poisons that smell sweet

and too often we are swept up
in the where, the why

that we don't realize
the decay has already set in too deep

The End

we assume we have
one more time, tomorrow

if I don't know
the length of my life

how can I measure
the good, the difficult

what is success?
and what is the point?

I wish I knew
what the end is

Heartbreak

everything seems so straight on the page
but in flesh and blood, rules go out the window

whether you leave me in this life
or if I find you in the next

heartbreak is inevitable
so feel it all

because one day you will be the one to leave
and all that's left is the ghost of your legacy

energy never leaves us
and pain in the absence of love is proof it was
there

Window Shopping

the beauty of fitting in
is often underrated

there's a certain relief to it
the ability to sink into a crowd and feel like you
belong

is disappearance freedom?
or hiding in plain sight

sometimes I wish I could fit
like a puzzle piece

feel community
and home

when will it be my turn
to stop trying on friends like window shopping

to use my battered key, hear the lock click
and be welcomed in

Sugar

begin to taste the sweetest offering
but the sugar turns sour when it hits my tongue

convince myself that it's an acquired taste
and there's still time

another day
another test

until bittersweet is a relief
a reprieve from the salt

I tell myself I don't crave it anymore
that I don't need it

but what parts of me are me
and which parts are you?

Or So They Say

"if it's really yours, it'll come back to you"
they say

so I let you go

and I see your skin through pictures
and remember how it felt against mine

but this is good for us

at least that's what I hear
and I cling to stories from our friends

your friends

rather than asking you to coffee
because we both know where that would lead

so I remain outside
with only glimpses through windows

and I remind myself

that I "deserve better"
or so they say

It Could Always Be Different

it could always be different

you leave home 2 minutes later
and miss the train

you stop for coffee
and feel the rain

it can be hard not to linger in the in-between
but one foot in front of the other
and you might move forward eventually

it could always be different
but why would you want it to be?

I Found You

of everyone in the world
what are the chances
that I found you

when the thunder
chases away all feeling

when my hands tremble
and storms threaten to swallow

when it feels like all is lost
and I lose my footing

in the midst of the chaos
there is always you.

People Pleaser

lately I've been feeling
selfish and crazy

my mind reminds me to think of others
to be polite and to please

sick of rearranging myself
to fit into impossible spaces

and when I look in the mirror at the monster I've
created
I love her

A Love Letter

maybe the beginning isn't
a time or a place

maybe the best place to start
is by forgiving yourself
and asking for forgiveness

Loss

loss isn't always sorrowful
sometimes it can be the most beautiful part

losing yourself
a loss of innocence

remember we cannot grow
if we cannot accept what is already done

In Every Lifetime

20

do you think
that we know each other in every lifetime

that every day for all eternity
it will be me and you

or is there a comfort
in knowing this is our only chance?

The Hero

what if
you believed in yourself
like you believed in magic

it never left you, you know
the hope of another dawn
the excitement of a new adventure

you are in every story
we heard as children
and now may be the perfect time to start

www.ingramcontent.com/pod-product-compliance
Lightning Source LLC
LaVergne TN
LVHW041302200726
843507LV00014B/3102